# MilesTalk

## Live Your Wildest Travel Dreams
## Using Miles and Points

D1600119

## DAVE GROSSMAN

Founder of MilesTalk.com

# CONTENTS

# CHAPTER 1

# How to Use this Book to Achieve Your Travel Dreams

Since 2003, I have collected literally **millions and millions** of **frequent flyer miles and hotel points**. I've flown around the world in **first class seats** that should have cost me **$29,000,** using only frequent flyer miles and a few bucks in tax. And I've stayed in some of the finest hotels, **all for *free***—thanks to points! I've hosted two seminars on miles and points at *South By Southwest* in Austin, and have been quoted in the *Wall Street Journal* and *Travel + Leisure*, published on Bravo TV's *JetSet* website, and spoken on the *Condé Nast Traveler* podcast series.

This book is an intro level summary of the tips and tricks you need to get started in the world of miles and points.

In this book, my goal is for you to understand what miles and points are (and the big difference between earning miles in an airline's own program versus points earned in transferable currencies.)

Once you understand what miles and points are, we'll talk about setting goals, followed by ways to earn miles and points and, then, how to spend them. And, at the end of the book, I'll provide a laundry list of great links you can use to feed your newfound addiction to miles and points.

I should note that there are two kinds of people in this hobby: those that accumulate miles and points for "aspirational redemptions," meaning first and business class flights and 5-star hotels you would never pay cash for, and those that just want as many free flights and nights as possible, and don't mind economy travel to do it, so long as it's free. Both are perfectly good reasons to collect miles and points, and both types of hobbyists will learn a lot from this book, but as I personally focus on the aspirational travel, you'll find a tilt towards that in the pages ahead.

For me, the flights and the hotels have become part of my travel experiences. Sure, I loved exploring Japan. But, instead of dreading the 14 hour flight there from New York in coach, I looked forward to sipping on $500 bottles of champagne and $100 wagyu steaks while lounging in my own suite on-board a Japan Airlines flight. I paid a grand total of $46 for that flight (and 160,000 American Airlines AAdvantage miles) avoiding a price tag of $29,000.

To whet your appetite, here is the seat on that JAL flight, along with some of the food and drink:

Japan Airlines First Class

I also recently rode up front in a Singapore Airlines Suite on their A380 airplane, where I had a closing door on my suite for the ultimate privacy in the air:

I spent 80,000 Chase Ultimate Rewards points for that ride from Frankfurt, Germany to NYC. And I could have earned those 80,000 points from just signing up for one credit card. But more on that later.

Adjoining Etihad First Class Apartments

# CHAPTER 2

# So, What are Miles and Points, Exactly?

When we hear the phrase "frequent flyer miles" we tend to think about airline miles where you would earn one mile for every mile flown. So if you flew from New York to London, you would earn 3,451 miles because that is how many miles the plane is flying. This traditional frequent flyer program was invented by American Airlines in May of 1981 just after airline deregulation. Other airlines quickly followed.

In this traditional type of frequent flyer program, one earns miles at the rate of one mile per mile flown and redeems them based on that airline's "Award Chart," which is generally zone-based. For example, if the airline prices a one-way business class flight award within North America at 25,000 miles, that is the price that will apply to any seats the airline makes available for frequent flyer redemption, whether the flight is New York to Miami (just 1,090 miles) or New York to Los Angeles (2,475 miles).

Unsurprisingly, this model led to what became known

among frequent flyers as "mileage runs," wherein miles addicts would take flights they did not need because the flight earned a lot of miles, relative to its fare. This still exists to a degree, but only works on certain airlines that still use traditional earning schemes and for earning airline "elite status," which, for now, is still based on flown miles in a calendar year, along with certain minimum spending requirements that make status harder and harder to earn by mileage run alone.

In 2018, the game has changed significantly. The big three airlines in the US: American Airlines, Delta Air Lines, and United Airlines, have all adopted a model wherein you now earn miles based on the price of your ticket. So while a $500 ticket that goes 8,000 miles round trip used to earn 8,000 miles, it may now only earn, for example, 5 miles per dollar or 2,500 miles.

Redemption of miles, on the other hand, remains tied to zones on most airlines. American and United both publish award charts that tell you how many miles you will need to redeem a flight from one region to another in Economy, Business, or First Class. Most global airlines do the same. Delta chooses not to publish award charts and instead requires you to enter the flights you want and pay whatever they tell you. In my opinion, this lack of transparency makes Delta's Skymiles less valuable than other airlines.

I call this model a "hybrid revenue-based model," meaning that you earn at a varying rate, according to fare, but still redeem at a fixed rate. Delta seems to be moving towards an entirely revenue based model, such as JetBlue and Southwest use, which I describe below. I'll discuss this more in Chapter 4.

The other major domestic US airlines are JetBlue, Southwest, and Alaska Airlines (which recently acquired

Virgin America.) JetBlue and Southwest both award frequent flyer points based on the cost of your ticket and you redeem based on the cost of your ticket. These are called "revenue-based points." On the one hand, it's nice to know what your points are worth, but, on the other hand, it takes all the fun out of it. One of the sweetest spots in this hobby has always been redeeming for the Premium cabins, First and Business, which cost many multiples of the cash price of economy, but generally only 2-3 times the cost in miles. In an entirely revenue-based program, however, you can't win that way. The cost in miles is always proportionate to the ticket price.

The one remaining program in the US that is still using the old style of fixed earning and redemption is Alaska Airlines. I suggest you look into them if they serve your market well as they have stellar customer service and some great partners for global mileage redemptions.

## Alliance Networks

Around the world, most airlines still use fixed earning and award charts and that is to your advantage. It means you will need to learn which airlines are in each alliance network. Note that most airlines also have partnerships beyond the alliances they are in. Alaska, for example, is not in any alliances but partners with Emirates, Cathay Pacific, Fiji Airways and more for both earning and spending miles.

American Airlines is in the Oneworld alliance, Delta Air Lines is in the SkyTeam alliance, and United Airlines is in the Star Alliance. This means that, in addition to any partnerships any airline you may travel on has, you can both credit flights to, and redeem your miles on, an alliance partner. When you redeem your miles, you use the award chart of the airline with which you have miles and make the booking with that same airline, but for travel on the partner airline.

Here's an example:

If you have American Airlines miles, as a Oneworld alliance member, you can redeem your American Airlines miles for a flight on on Japan Airlines (JAL), which is also a Oneworld member. The cost of the award will be based on whatever award chart American Airlines publishes. So, if their award chart says a First Class flight between North America and Japan is 80,000 miles, you can call American Airlines and tell them you would like to book a flight on Japan Airlines. People always ask how you "transfer the miles to the other airline," but you don't transfer anything anywhere. The airline where you have your miles banked takes care of issuing the ticket for you on the other airline. These days you can do many bookings for partner awards online, but many still require a phone call. Knowing which those are and how to check availability is something that you learn over time. In Chapter 6, I'll talk more about what tools you can use to find more award availability than the general public can easily find.

## Points vs. Miles

Points encompass all airline frequent flyer programs that don't use miles for either earning or spending miles, all hotel loyalty programs, and all credit card programs where banks issue their proprietary points.

Interestingly, while Capital One uses the term *miles* for their travel card line, they aren't really miles at all. They are points that are redeemed for travel, based on a fixed value per point, and tied to the cost of the ticket. They really should be termed points.

Examples of credit card programs are American Express' *Membership Rewards*™, Chase's *Ultimate Rewards*™, and Citi's *ThankYou*™ points.

Points can always be exchanged for value in some way. At their most basic level, they can be redeemed for a statement credit. But in this book we will only discuss points that can be redeemed or transferred for enough value to be worth our time. I'll note here that it's simple to get a credit card that will give you a straight 2% cash back, so for us to care we need to be getting more than 2% in value from our points. Capital One's program can't.

In Chapters 8 and 9, we will talk about the four major programs with transferable points, programs I refer to as Transferable Currency. This is because the sweetest spots in award travel are still available using frequent flyer miles and these programs can transfer the points you earn into many different frequent flyer programs, where you can redeem those miles for First and Business Class flights.

# CHAPTER 3

# Elite Status with Airlines and Hotels: Is It Worth It?

W hile this book isn't specifically about elite perks, it's important for any hobbyist to know what this is, so you can make an informed decision about whether or not you want to care. It's also very useful to understand *Status Matches*, as they can exponentially multiply programs in which you have status.

## Airline Status

Airline status is earned based on how much you fly. Makes sense, right? Each program has a series of tiers that comes along with some predefined benefits to treat you "extra special." The idea is that, because you enjoy the perks of status, you will fly that one airline over all others. The most basic perks of status almost always come from flying 25,000 miles in a year. From there you will likely hit another status tier after 50,000, 75,000, 100,000, and/or 125,000 flown miles in one calendar year.

You will generally get miles that count towards your qualifying status by flying, not just that airline, but any of its alliance partners (or other partners). For example, if you are loyal to American Airlines, you will also earn miles that count towards status when flying any Oneworld airline, such as British Airways or LAN, and crediting those flights to American.

Perks at the lowest tier generally include things like access to "premium" seats, including seats that are closer to the front of the plane, aisle and window seats, free checked bags, and, sometimes, upgrades to premium economy or business class. As you get higher up in Elite status, you get prioritized for upgrades and generally get access to some fee waivers. You may be able to change your flight the same day for no charge, cancel an award for no charge, or waive a booking fee for booking an award close to the date of travel. You'll also earn more frequent flyer miles for paid fares when you have status. If you are curious about the exact details of status with a particular airline, their website will make clear how you earn status levels and what your benefits are.

Also, keep in mind that most airlines have affinity credit cards that, in exchange for a small annual fee, will give you most of the benefits of a low tier status, including free checked bags and priority boarding. None include upgrades, but some high end credit cards do include a way to earn elite status qualifying miles for spend levels. If you value elite status, that is a hack worth knowing.

### Airline Credit Cards

Here is how it works with a Delta Platinum Skymiles Credit Card from American Express, which has an annual fee: When you spend $25,000 in a calendar year, you earn

10,000 Delta Medallion Qualifying Miles (MQM). When you spend another $25,000 you get a second 10,000 MQMs. Delta Silver Medallion status (the lowest tier) requires 25,000 MQMs earned in a year. If you had this credit card and spent $50,000 a year on it, you'd only need to fly 5,000 miles in a year to achieve Silver Medallion status. Better yet, there is a second Delta credit card called the Reserve, which allows you to earn 15,000 MQMs after each of the first two blocks of $30,000 you spend on the card (i.e. you can earn up to 30,000 MQMs). If you had both cards and spent $50,000 on the Platinum and $60,000 on the Reserve you would earn 50,000 MQMs, which would actually earn you mid-tier Gold Status.

Is that worthwhile? To some. Keep in mind that you only get the benefits when actually flying the airline. So while it probably would not be worthwhile for someone that earns very few flown miles to pay the annual fees involved with having the credit cards, plus put that much spend on a card earning just 1 cent per mile, it may make sense for someone earning 25,000 flown miles (Silver status on Delta) to do the above to "upgrade" to Platinum status and reap the additional upgrades on their paid flights.

## Hotel Status

You won't be surprised to learn that hotel status works much the same way as airline status. By staying a certain number of nights at one chain, you will earn status that entitles you to things like early check-in / late checkout, free breakfast, bonus loyalty points, room upgrades, and, at the highest levels, upgrades to suites.

Like airline alliances, your programs aren't limited to stays in one brand, but rather one chain. In this case, one hotel company owns multiple brands in their portfolio and you can earn and spend points when you stay at any hotel within that portfolio. As an example, Marriott owns not only Marriott hotels, but also Courtyard, Residence Inn, Springhill Suites, and many more. Marriott's loyalty program is called Marriott Rewards. Staying at any of these hotels will earn you points in the Marriott Rewards program and you can similarly redeem your points for free nights at any of these brands.

## Lifetime Status

Many airlines and hotels offer "Lifetime Status," after you have flown enough miles or slept in enough of their beds. You can check with your preferred airline or chain to see if they offer this just by Googling "[airline or hotel chain] lifetime status." It's meant to be a perk that rewards career-long loyalty with the ability to enjoy those benefits after you retire. There used to be shortcuts to earning lifetime status. For instance, some airline programs used to count all earned miles from any source towards the million miles needed for lifetime status, but they all now will require some real loyalty by getting your butt in their seats or beds.

## Status Matches

Status matches are a great way to stretch your elite statuses. A status match simply means asking one loyalty program to match the status you have earned with another one. And a lot of the time, they will!

Why do they do this? Because if you fly enough with one airline or stay enough with one hotel chain, you can be sure there is another one that would love to earn your business.

So let's say you have Platinum status with airline X. Airline Y knows how many miles that means you fly. So they will offer you status to try out their product in a truly comparable way. You see, when you have status it's a bit painful to fly or stay where you have none. The "match" ensures you get to sample their equivalent product with the hopes that you will earn it the hard way the following year.

Matches come in various forms. Sometimes, you will get a trial status for a few months, during which time you have to earn a prorated portion of a normal year's requirement to get it for the full year. Sometimes they are an outright full match for a full program year completely gratis. Usually the match is free, but not always. Notably, American Airlines charges a fee to enroll in one of their Gold or Platinum status challenges and they call it a challenge rather than a match.

Status matches can be a great way to kick the can down the curb when you know you won't re-qualify for another year. Let's say you are halfway through the year with your Delta Gold Medallion Status. You know you won't requalify but maybe you'll be flying some other airline a lot soon. Or not. See which programs will work for your travel needs and are offering a match. Status Matcher (http://www.statusmatcher.com) is a good place to see where you'll have the most luck.

## Promotions

This is more of a Public Service Announcement: Always opt-in to marketing emails from the loyalty programs you care about and follow not just MilesTalk, but a range of miles and points websites and bloggers to make sure you aren't leaving any points on the table.

Hotel chains often have quarterly promotions that include offers like double/triple bonus points, stay twice and get a night free, or stay a certain number of nights to get a bunch of bonus points. Some offers can definitely spur you to choose a hotel in one chain versus another, so be sure you are on the lookout. Always double check, however, that the hotel you intend to stay at is "participating," as there are rare exceptions where you assume that a property is participating, but the fine print excludes that property. I notice this a lot on Starwood Preferred Guest (SPG) promotions.

Airlines will often have similar bonus mile offers for flying a particular route they are trying to increase awareness of. Car rental companies have these as well. Subscribe to all their marketing emails so you don't miss out.

# CHAPTER 4

# Setting your Travel Goals (Earn and Burn)

This is probably the most important chapter in the book, so you'll want to pay extra attention here.

The goal of this hobby is not to build your balances into millions of points in each program. Some people have the misguided goal of trying to save up all their miles for retirement, so they can travel the world for free in their golden years. Sounds great, right?

Just one small problem. Frequent flyer miles suffer from the worst kind of inflation over time. Not only do they *not* earn interest, like cash in the bank would, but the frequent flyer programs continually devalue the miles by raising the goalposts for awards. What is a 25,000 mile redemption opportunity today could be a 375,000 mile redemption in 20 years. Or, with the way things are going with US airlines lately, by the time you finish this book. It's in all of their terms and conditions that they can do whatever they want whenever they want, so all you can do is know about it.

When you play a short term game, you are more likely

to have the goalposts stay where they are. Some devaluations happen with a few months of notice given to members, allowing you to book some future flights or hotel nights in advance at "old levels." Others happen with no notice at all. With a short term horizon, your odds are much better.

This is why it is so important to first define your goals. Why are you collecting the miles and points? If you are looking for two round trip tickets to Asia in First Class, you'll have a very different strategy than a family of 4 looking to get to Disney in the cheapest way possible.

It's also important to know the difference between international First Class and Business Class. Many airlines, such as Delta, have moved away from true First Class products internationally and have Economy, Premium Economy, and Business Class as their highest class of service. Other airlines, for now, still have true First Class, which is always a very large seat or suite, top notch food and service, and, generally, only a handful of other passengers in the cabin. Newer planes such as the Airbus A350 are commonly being ordered without First Class, so if that is something that is important for you to experience, you'll need to spend some time researching which airline products you want to try and what miles and points will get you on board. Something else that is important to keep in mind is that if you are hoarding Delta Skymiles, they cannot be used to book international First Class with any of their partners. So if you were hoping to fly Skyteam partners Air France or Korean Air in First, your Skymiles can't get you there. In fact, Korean Air requires you use their own miles for First Class, so you can transfer in from a credit card for that. And Air France not only requires you to use their Flying Blue miles, but you need Flying Blue status as well. Meanwhile, both American and United still have their own First Class cabins on some international flights and their miles can book you into First Class on their partners (with some caveats.)

Knowing the airlines you are likely to use (and class of service you want) means you can narrow down the types of miles or points you need for your goal. If you are trying to fly domestically for four people in coach, you'll probably want to strategize to get enough points for a Companion Pass on Southwest (where the companion pays only taxes on a second ticket unlimited times for the duration of the pass, including on award tickets.) You can earn the pass from just two credit card signup bonuses and, timed strategically, you can even have it for two full years. But if you want to fly to Asia in First Class, you'll be looking at which partners serve the markets you want to fly to for the least amount of miles. A website called Award Hacker (http://awardhacker.com) will help guide you in the right direction. It won't tell you what kind of availability each program has, however.

Let's say you find that ANA (All Nippon Airways, a Japanese airline) would be a great airline for your goals. Your next step is to check the availability for the season you would want to go. ANA availability could be checked by creating an account on their system, or using United's website or Air Canada's Aeroplan website to search as they will also show ANA availability in all classes. If you find that there is reasonable availability around the time frame you will want (understanding that the exact dates you want may not be available by the time you have enough points) you can move to the step of acquiring the right points. But first, we need to understand all the ways we can get the flights we want.

Let's workshop an example. (Note that, by the time you read this, award rates may have changed and opportunities to redeem from other programs with ANA may have changed, so check current info):

**Travel goal:** Fly from New York, NY, USA to Tokyo, Japan round-trip in First Class next September.

**Best options:** Both *ANA* (from above) and *Japan Airlines (JAL)* would be excellent choices, as they both fly non-stop three-class flights from NYC to Tokyo.

**Best programs for redeeming on each:** Here's where we fire up Award Hacker. Our best options are 140,000 JAL miles, 140,000 Alaska miles (to redeem on JAL) or 150,000 miles to redeem on ANA with ANA miles. You could also redeem other Star Alliance carrier's miles on ANA, but none would be less than these amounts. This same award using United miles (for the ANA flights) would be 220,000 United miles (110,000 each way).

In this case we also run across an exception. Virgin Atlantic miles, as of Dec 2017, can be used to fly ANA round trip from NYC-Tokyo at a rate of 120,000 miles round trip. This is not listed at AwardHacker.

**Availability: (Please see Chapter 6 for a more in-depth look at finding availability)**

First I use United.com to check availability on ANA.

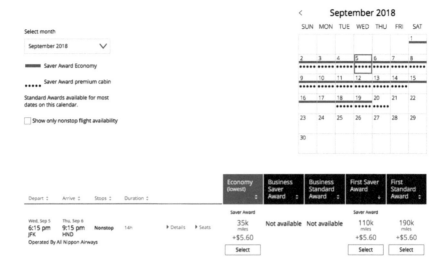

I check some dates in my timeframe of next September and find plenty of flights at the First Saver level (110k miles each way on United.) Remember, this is just so I know ANA has availability. I'm not actually going to book it here.

Next, I want to see what kind of availability Japan Airlines has, so I can decide which goal to plan for.

The best way to see Japan Airlines availability at a glance for a whole month is on the JAL website. So we will create a frequent flyer account with JAL and login.

The JAL Mileage bank website lets me view a month at a glance. I easily find out that for next September, there's almost no 1st class availability, but there is plenty of Business Class space. The black diamond means no space, while a circle indicates a seat.

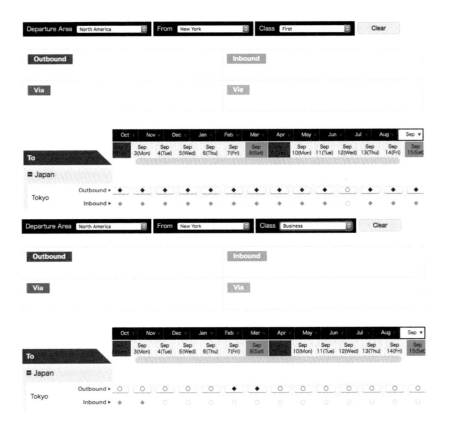

I have a decision to make now. I can reconsider if I really care about 1st class. Maybe Business Class is enough? Checking back over at AwardHacker, I learn that I could fly this same route in Business Class roundtrip for 85k miles on ANA or 100k miles on JAL. Or 120k miles using American Airlines AAdvantage miles, should I already have a stash of those. I'm tempted, and in real life I might change course here, especially if trying for more than one ticket.

But let's continue our example, assuming we are set on 1st Class. ANA is our clear winner. So now we know we want to acquire the miles to fly ANA and the best way to do this will be using either ANA's own miles or Virgin Atlantic miles.

Next step: How easy/hard is it to earn each of those miles? There are going to be two main routes to look at.

1) Credit card sign-up bonuses.
2) Transfer partners. Remember, we need either 120,000 Virgin Atlantic or 140,000 ANA miles.

Let's check credit cards. There's a Virgin Atlantic credit card that at this moment will net 20,000 miles for signing up. That's not much, but it's something. ANA's credit card is much worse: just 5,000 bonus miles for a new card.

Now we'll check transfer partners. I maintain a post with "what transfers where" (http://milestalk.com/transfer-partners/) and I'll reference that. I see that American Express Membership Rewards and SPG both transfer to ANA. But more interestingly, I see that every major transferable currency (Chase, Amex, Citi, and SPG) all transfer to Virgin.

Boom! We now know we are going to use Virgin Atlantic to book our flights (and hope they don't drop ANA as a booking partner between the time we start planning and when we have enough points to book!!).

We can either get the Virgin Atlantic credit card for 20k and then find another 100k from a transferable points partner, or partners, or get the whole 120k from a transferable points partner, or partners.

Since Virgin Atlantic is a transfer partner of everyone, we can actually do this by opening a few key credit cards that, with some minimum spend, will get us the 120,000 points we need.

Here's the plan I'd craft, based on today's cards and signup bonuses. Keep in mind that bonuses come and go and can be very high one day and almost nothing the next, so you'll have to look at all the cards and see what makes sense for you.

a) If you have a small business, this is really simple. One Chase Sapphire Reserve card (50,000 Chase Ultimate Rewards signup bonus with $4,000 in spend in 3 months) and one Chase Business Preferred card (80,000 point signup bonus with $5,000 in spend in 3 months). That's 130,000 bonus points, plus what you earn from the minimum spend, for a total of 139,000 points. We have 19,000 to spare! Transfer 120,000 to Virgin Atlantic, call Virgin to book, and I'm done (after rechecking actual dates of availability, of course, since exact flight availability changes minute by minute.)

b) No small business? Open one Chase Sapphire Reserve card (or Sapphire Preferred) for 50,000 bonus points and one Citi ThankYou Premier card (50,000 point bonus) as well as the Virgin Atlantic card for a total of 120,000 points. Alternatively, just get the two cards with the 50,000 points each and spend the additional money on the cards to get to 120,000 total. You could also look for high bonus offers on American Express Membership Rewards cards (there can be 100,000 point offers for the Platinum card and 75,000 bonus points on the Gold card on occasion.) The Starwood Preferred Guest credit cards are also an option.

Plan complete! I'm now ready to spend my new found points on a round trip First Class flight of a lifetime!

Now, I can start planning my next travel goal. *Earn and Burn!*

It's worth noting too, that once you start using the right

rewards credit cards, you can accumulate a lot of points just by spending your normal monthly expenses on the right cards. The Chase Sapphire Reserve, for example, earns 3x points on all of your travel and dining spend. If you spend $2,000 a month on travel (this includes airfare, hotels, parking and even Uber) and dining expenses and put those charges on your Reserve, you'll earn 72,000 Chase Ultimate Rewards points a year! So please don't get the idea that signup bonuses are the only way to get points. They provide a great start and introduce you to new cards, but bonus category spend is a fantastic way to rack up transferable currency.

Etihad First Class Apartment Beds

# CHAPTER 5

# Airline Miles and Alliances: How They Work and How to Work Them

Now that we've done a deep dive into a practical example to get you to see how easy it can be to make this hobby work for you, let's take a step back.

It's very important to understand how airlines partner with one another as that is a key to both earning more miles "the hard way," as well as redeeming your hard-earned miles. When I say, "the hard way," I'm referring to: with your butt in an airplane seat, rather than by earning miles via spending on credit cards. These are playfully referred to as butt-in-seat miles, as opposed to miles earned by credit cards and other methods.

There are three global airline alliances: Oneworld, SkyTeam, and Star Alliance. Each of the three US global carriers belongs to one of these. American Airlines is part of Oneworld, Delta Air Lines is part of SkyTeam, and United Airlines is part of the Star Alliance.

Most people in the US will have a preference towards one of the big three carriers, whether it's because they have the most flights from your home airport or some other reason. Therefore, it's very important to know which other airlines around the world are in the same alliance, so you can maximize your rewards. In some cases, you may even realize that it makes more sense to select a new preferred airline, based on how well you can redeem your miles for the trips you want.

Below is a current summary of which airlines are in each major alliance.

**Oneworld**: American Airlines, British Airways, Finnair, Iberia, Qantas, Japan Airlines (JAL), Cathay Pacific, LATAM, Qatar, Royal Jordanian, S7 Airlines, Malaysia Airlines, SriLankan Airlines

**SkyTeam**: Delta, Air France, KLM, Korean Air, Alitalia, AeroMexico, Aeroflot, Air Europa, Czech Airlines, China Airlines, China Eastern, China Southern, Aerolineas Argentinas, Garuda Indonesia, Xiamen Airlines, Kenya Airways, TAROM, Vietnam Airlines, Saudia, Middle East Airlines

**Star Alliance**: United, Air Canada, Austrian, Asiana, Lufthansa, Singapore Airlines, South African Airways, SWISS, Brussels, Avianca, Thai Airways, TAP Portugal, Turkish Airlines, LOT Polish, SAS, Air New Zealand, Adria Airways, Aegean Airlines, Air China, Air India, All Nippon Airways (ANA), Avianca, Croatia Airlines, Ethiopian Airlines, EVA Air, Shenzhen Airlines

Aside from the standard alliances, always check the website of your preferred airline to see which non-alliance partners they have. For example, Etihad, which has one of the best First Class products in the sky, partners with American Airlines, despite not being in Oneworld. So you can both earn and redeem American Airlines AAdvantage miles on Etihad. Alaska Airlines is another great example. They are not currently in any alliance, yet they have a wide range of partners for both earning and redeeming their miles.

## Where To Credit Your Paid Flights

This is a bit advanced, but I wanted to include it. Remember that, depending on the airline you are crediting your miles to, it may be based not just on the cost of your flight or the number of miles flown, but also the fare bucket you are booked in. To most, a "fare bucket" doesn't mean anything. But they are important to know about because they will dictate the miles you earn and it could be anywhere from only 25% of your flown miles to as much as 500%!

A "fare bucket" describes the many inventory slots that an airline uses to sell the same seat. Let's look at a hypothetical flight from JFK to LAX on American Airlines. They are showing the following inventory to travel agents (and is available to you if you use a paid service like ExpertFlyer.com):

F7 A4 J7 D7 I0 Y7 B7 H7 K7 M7 L7
G7 V7 S7 N7 Q7 O7 E7

The F7 means that 7 or more First Class seats are for sale at full fare. A4 means 4 seats are for sale in First class at a discounted rate. If you book full fare First Class, your fare basis will be "F."

J7 / D7 / I0 means that 7 or more seats are for sale at both full fare business class and discounted business class, but none at their biggest discount business class fare.

The rest are coach inventory buckets. A nicely complex 13 buckets for the SAME coach seat. A "Y" fare is the most expensive coach ticket and is generally refundable. "O" is the cheapest discount fare. "E" is for Employee travel and for same day flight changes.

Now, even though all of those 13 coach fare buckets give you the same coach seat, they will earn you different amounts of miles. If you credit to American, it won't dictate how many miles you earn (although higher fares earn more elite qualifying miles). On American, you'll earn by the fare you paid. Logically, though, higher fare classes generally cost more.

But what if you credit the flights to other Oneworld airlines?

We head over to the website *WhereToCredit.com* to find out.

Let's say we are booked on a deep discount O fare and the flight is 4,000 miles. You paid $200. Where To Credit will inform us that if we credit to Etihad or Finnair, we'll get a full 4,000 miles credited. But British Airways Iberia would only give us 1,000 miles! Without any status on AA, if you credit the miles to AA itself, you would earn 5 miles per dollar or 1,000 miles.

Of course, it doesn't necessarily make sense to credit to the best earning partner, because you need to build up a balance you can redeem! But if you look at your flying pattern, you may find a better place to credit than you are today.

When you are flying paid first or business fares (lucky you!) the multipliers can be huge. A full fare British Airways (F booking code) will net you 500% of flown miles when credited to Alaska Airlines. That's right - a 6,000 mile round trip flight would earn you a whopping 30,000 Alaska miles! Credited to American Airlines, that same flight earns only 9,000 AAdvantage miles.

## Redeeming Your Miles On An Alliance Partner Or Partner Airline

When you have miles with a member of one of the alliances, you can, with some rare exceptions, redeem them on any of those other carriers.

As mentioned in the Travel Goals example in Chapter 4, we can use our miles to book award travel, not just with the airline with which we have our miles, but also with any of their alliance partners or other partner airlines. So, for example, United, Lufthansa, and Singapore Airlines are all in the Star Alliance. If I have United miles, I can redeem for any of these three airlines, as well as any other Star Alliance airlines. I'll be using the United Airlines award chart to determine how many miles a particular route will cost, and then either use the United website, or call United directly, to check availability and book the flight.

This applies equally if I have my stash of miles on Singapore Airlines or Avianca or Air Canada. Often, the award price of the same flight on the same airline costs very different amounts of miles based on what program's miles you book it with.

For example, if you want to book a Lufthansa 1st class award from the US to Europe right now it would cost you 110,000 United miles or just 80,000 Singapore Airlines miles. If you have miles in both programs, or can transfer to both programs from transferable currency, you can take advantage of this. I call this "*frequent flyer mile arbitrage.*"

You can easily see now why it would be better to earn miles on a transferable currency credit card than on a United Airlines credit card. You'll have options.

## Dynamic Award Pricing: A Growing Risk Towards Aspirational Award Travel

There is a growing trend in recent years towards dynamic award pricing, the term for tying the cost of an award ticket tightly to the cost of the equivalent revenue ticket – generally at around 1 cent per mile. So a $500 ticket would cost 50,000 miles.

*This is bad for us miles junkies for two reasons:*

The first reason applies to everyone that uses miles, and it is that this move basically makes it pointless to earn miles from credit card spending. You see, you generally earn miles (or points that transfer to miles) at around 1 to 1.5 miles per dollar (setting aside category bonuses for a minute here). If the best that you can redeem for is a penny per mile, wouldn't you have been better off just earning 2% cash back? Probably.

The second reason is that many of us go out of our way to earn points for aspirational awards in First or Business class. These tickets cost many, many multiples of coach in most cases, but only 2-3x the cost in miles. This allows a sort of symbiosis where airlines that can't sell those pricey tickets can remove miles from their accounting ledger and we get a great deal, sometimes even an experience of a lifetime in a private suite on board a plane.

When you move to revenue based awards, that $10,000 first class ticket is no longer, for example, 110,000 miles. It's now 1,000,000 (ONE MILLION) miles.

Does this make sense for the airlines? Well, it's easy to see how the bean counters think so. If you redeem one million miles for that ticket instead of 110,000 miles, they reduce their liability by more than 9 times.

Let's just say that if all the airlines in the world went this route, it would become very hard to find value in accumulating miles from credit card spending.

# CHAPTER 6

# Finding Availability for Airline Awards: They're Hiding In Plain Sight

One of the hardest parts about this hobby can be redeeming for award travel when you want it and for as many passengers as you need it. While there is no voodoo magic that will make award seats appear out of nowhere (believe me, I've tried!), there are a lot of things the average traveler doesn't know about, leaving some room for the informed traveler (my readers!) to have better odds.

The first thing to know is that no matter how much you know, there will always be some routes, especially at certain times of year, on some airlines that are extremely rare to find. Real First Class will generally be easier to find when you only need one seat, simply because there are so few seats. You may find two, but if you are two people, you may have to "settle" for Business Class. That doesn't mean you can't find two First Class seats or even 4 Business Class seats, it just means that the more you are asking for the harder it will be to actually find. Trying for 2 Business Class tickets from North America to Australia or New Zealand around the New Year? GOOD

LUCK! It may happen, but you won't find those seats by doing one casual search or lazily calling your airline of choice. No, you'll need every tip and trick at your disposal to even have a chance on that one.

To find the best options for your route, I like to use Google Flights (http://google.com/flights) just to see what airlines serve the route I want non-stop. It helps me narrow down my first choice options. If you strike out on all the non-stops, or they don't exist from your home market, you'll want to start looking at connections, but non-stops are going to be your best starting point.

Once you know what airlines best serve your market, it's time to check availability.

As a general rule of thumb, you can use the following websites to search online availability:

> **Oneworld:** British Airways or Qantas
> **Skyteam:** Air France, then Delta
> **Star Alliance:** Air Canada or United

Each of these sites, however, will have a bunch of airlines not included in search results.

**Exceptions:**

- British Airways won't show Aer Lingus (use United to check Aer Lingus) or Alaska Airlines (use Alaska's site to search Alaska Airlines awards).
- You can redeem American Airlines and Delta miles for travel on Air Tahiti Nui, which can be great for trips to Tahiti or Australia/New Zealand from the US West Coast. But there is no way to find availability

online, unless you use the paid service ExpertFlyer. More on ExpertFlyer in a bit.

- To search Etihad award space, create an account on the Etihad website.
- Two airlines Air France will show online, but Delta will not, are Xiamen Airlines (China) and Czech Airlines.
- Use Qantas (or ExpertFlyer) to find award space on Emirates.
- 1st Class awards on Singapore Airlines, Korean Air, and Air France all need to be searched on their respective website as no partner miles can redeem for them.
- Delta miles can not be redeemed for International 1st Class in any carrier at any time.

No doubt, this is where it starts to get very confusing for some people. You need to keep track of where you have miles, what airlines are in each alliance, and then you have to know where to search availability! It can make your head spin. Just remember that, the harder something is, the more value there is in mastering it! If I, or anyone else, could make this all super easy, there'd be no award space left for any of us. Not that we wouldn't make it super easy if we could, but we can't, and in the end that works to your advantage. You're already putting in the time to read this book and you'll come out the other side of this with some amazing trips.

Let's use a few examples to help train your thought process.

## Example 1:

| | |
|---|---|
| **You want:** | a First or Business class flight on Cathay Pacific |
| **You have:** | American Airlines miles |
| **You know:** | American and Cathay Pacific are both in Oneworld |
| **You also know:** | You can't search Cathay Pacific availability on AA.com, but you can find it on BA.com or Qantas. |
| **You then:** | Search BA.com and find flights you want |
| **And then:** | You call American Airlines, say you want to redeem your miles for a Cathay Pacific flight, and then feed them the flights you already found available on BA.com. |
| **And if:** | The agent can't find those flights that you are almost certain are available, you HUCA (Hang Up and Call Again) and politely ask the next agent to try and locate the available flights. |
| **Finally:** | You have an amazing trip booked! |

## Example 2:

| | |
|---|---|
| **You want:** | a Business class flight on Air New Zealand from Sydney to Auckland |
| **You have:** | United Airlines miles |
| **You know:** | United and Air New Zealand are both in Star Alliance |

**You also know:**  You can simply use United.com to search availability. That's easy!

**Example 3: (this is a harder one)**

**You want:**  A Business Class flight to Shenzhen, China from New York

**You have:**  Delta Skymiles

**You know:**  Shenzhen flies the route non-stop, but you also know that Delta.com won't show you availability.

**You use:**  Either ExpertFlyer or AirFrance.com to search availability

**You find:**  A seat available on the date you want on the AirFrance.com website

**The hard part:**  You now have to call Delta on the phone and find an agent that knows how to book a partner award that isn't in their integrated booking system. You call and feed them the exact flights that AirFrance.com shows available. They say they can't find it. You HUCA. You may even have to HUCA multiple times. At some point, if AirFrance.com is still showing the flights as available you should be able to find an agent to book it.

| | |
|---|---|
| **The possible exception:** | There is a term "phantom availability" that describes an airline showing a flight as available, even though it's actually not. In this case, assuming Air France was showing the phantom availability and you tried to actually book it, there you would receive an error. This is why, when you are transferring over credit card points to book a flight, you may want to call the airline first and confirm that the agents see the availability. It's rare, but it does happen where you see a seat and move the points, only to get an error at the end. It's one of the most frustrating technology glitches in this game, but know that when that happens, the phone agent is generally powerless to remedy it. |

## ExpertFlyer

ExpertFlyer.com is a fantastic "advanced user" tool for award availability. It will show you availability for a particular route and airline over as many as 6 days at once. It does require a paid subscription of about $10 a month.

Let's say I want to find out if I can get from New York (JFK) to London (LHR) in Business on American Airlines next week. I go to "Awards & Upgrades," enter JFK and LHR as my cities and AA as my airline. I select the date +/- 3 days and search for Business class, which ExpertFlyer lets me know is "U" class inventory in case I don't already know that.

I learn that there are no non-stops available, but if I can get myself to Raleigh, there's one seat there tomorrow. It's also an easy tabbed layout to see my options. AA.com happens to also be pretty good, though it wouldn't have shown me the Raleigh option, unless there was also an award seat from JFK-RDU. With other airlines that don't let you see a month at a time for an award search, it's more valuable.

**Departing Flights**
Search Departing JFK on 10/30/17 12:00 AM ± 3 Day(s) for LHR
Flying AA on booking class U

Legend: Create Flight Alert, View Flight Details, View Seat Map

Departing 10/27/17 to 11/02/17

| Flight | Stops | Depart | Arrive | Aircraft | Frequency Reliability | Description | Code | Seats |
|---|---|---|---|---|---|---|---|---|
| 0 Connections | | | | | | | | |
| AA 100 | 0 | JFK 10/27/17 8:20 PM | LHR 10/28/17 8:20 AM | 77W | Daily 74% / 33m | Business - MileSAAver Award (Including 2-Cabin Domestic First) | U | 0 |
| 0 Connections | | | | | | | | |
| AA 106 | 0 | JFK 10/27/17 8:10 PM | LHR 10/28/17 8:10 AM | 772 | Daily 68% / 26m | Business - MileSAAver Award (Including 2-Cabin Domestic First) | U | 0 |
| 0 Connections | | | | | | | | |
| AA 104 | 0 | JFK 10/27/17 10:29 PM | LHR 10/28/17 10:30 AM | 772 | Daily 68% / 38m | Business - MileSAAver Award (Including 2-Cabin Domestic First) | U | 0 |
| 1 Connections | | | | | | | | |
| AA 4362 | 0 | JFK 10/27/17 2:55 PM | RDU 10/27/17 4:43 PM | ER4 | Daily 65% / 27m | | | |
| AA 174 | 0 | RDU 10/27/17 6:10 PM | LHR 10/28/17 6:35 AM | 772 | Daily 82% / 60m | Business - MileSAAver Award (Including 2-Cabin Domestic First) | U | 1 |
| 1 Connections | | | | | | | | |
| AA 4630 | 0 | JFK 10/27/17 5:00 PM | BOS 10/27/17 6:22 PM | E75 | Daily 45% / 54m | Business - MileSAAver Award (Including 2-Cabin Domestic First) | U | 0 |
| AA (BA) 6200 | 0 | BOS 10/27/17 9:35 PM | LHR 10/28/17 9:10 AM | 747 | Daily 90% / 35m | | | |

But the real value in ExpertFlyer isn't in the general search. It's the ability to have ExpertFlyer monitor a particular flight I want (or more than one, though you set each alert individually) and alert me when there is a seat available. That's right, if I'm looking for a rare Business class seat to Sydney, for example, I can figure out all the flights that would work for me and then have it notify me when (if) availability opens up.

For example, if I have American Airlines AAdvantage miles, my options to Australia include AA from LA to Sydney or Qantas from LA or Dallas to Sydney, or LA to Melbourne.

I'll pick a flight, let's say DFW to SYD and +/- 3 days from March 3rd. I do a standard award search:

In this case, we see 9 or more seats in coach available, but nothing on any of these days in Business. So I'll set an alert by pressing the ! graphic on the right. I set an alert name I'll remember and submit.

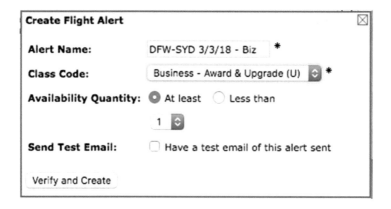

And one bonus tip: Your cell phone carrier has a special way to format your phone number as an email address. For T-Mobile, it's yournumber@tmomail.net. I use this to get text alerts for my flight notifications. You want your alerts ASAP when there's availability, because seats on coveted routes don't last long!

ExpertFlyer has some other great features that you can explore, such as seat alerts. You just booked a flight and there are no window seats now? Set an alert so you know when one opens up!

Sign up at <u>ExpertFlyer.com</u> and take a look around. They offer a free trial as well.

# CHAPTER 7

# Hotel Points: Luxury on Landing

Hotel points are a very different animal from airline miles, but very valuable in different ways. Your two main reasons to collect any particular hotel points are a) to redeem them for expensive hotel stays, and b) to transfer them to airline miles (select programs only).

In general, the goal of hotel points is to to get free nights. But, just like I don't think you should kill yourself to earn 50,000 airline miles to redeem them for $500 in flights, I think the same way about hotel points.

A very important thing to remember is that all hotel points are not created equal. Just like some airline miles are more valuable than others (because of their rewards charts or availability), some hotel points are more or less valuable than others.

It's easy to be fooled. A signup bonus for 100,000 Hilton points, for example, may seem way better than one for 35,000 SPG Starpoints. But what is each bonus worth? Well, based on things like versatility (SPG can transfer to almost any airline at 1:25 to 1, while Hilton would transfer to most airlines at 10 points for just 1 mile) and how many points for a free night (Hilton standard awards can hit 90,000 while SPG's top out, with a few exceptions, at 35,000), we easily see they aren't equal. In fact, I value a Hilton point at around 4/10 of a cent while I value Starpoints at between 2 and 2.5 cents apiece.

Then there is availability. Does your preferred chain have a "no blackout" policy? While no blackouts doesn't mean there's always a room for points, it certainly helps. My best redemptions have been at peak demand times.

To decide which hotel's points (and you can favor more than one!) is best for you, you will have to consider how you earn your points (credit card or actual hotel nights) as well as how you plan to redeem the points, nights or flights.

To me, redeeming hotel points at times of high demand when rates are high is the best way to use hotel points. I sure hate paying 5x the price for a room just because it's New Year's Eve. But if I can find rooms available for points, they will match up to the category rate for that hotel. If it's 20,000 points a night on Dec 15th, it's probably 20,000 points on Dec 31st as well, even though the cash rate may be many multiples of normal.

**Award categories:** Check your preferred hotel chain's loyalty program to see how you redeem nights with them. Most use a system not unlike an airline's award chart to define various levels of hotel categories, assigning a price to each. Let's say a chain has 7 categories of hotels. They will have a chart that says a night costs a certain amount of their points at each level. And, like airlines, this is where you can arbitrage your points to extract the most value. Don't use points at times of low demand. Use cash then, and save your points for times when the rates are higher.

**Exceptions:** *Hilton Honors* has gone from a fixed award chart to one that changes based on the cost of the room for your nights, essentially revenue-based. But they seem to cap the upper limits at the levels of the most recent award chart, meaning you can still get multiples of value during high demand times as long as there are "standard" rooms for sale.

**No blackouts:** Remember that in almost all instances, even a "No Blackouts" promise refers only to the lowest level room type for any hotel. And they may only sell 4 base level rooms, categorizing everything else as a better room type. Hotels do often play games to try and avoid selling you that $1,000 a night room for points and that's just part of the sport. It works out enough of the time to still be very worthwhile to collect hotel points.

## Booking Direct Vs Booking With An Online Agency (OTA) Like Expedia Or Orbitz

The most important thing to know is that when you book via a third party website (anything other than the hotel brand's own website) you are most likely not going to earn any hotel points nor receive elite member benefits for that stay. For that reason, if you can get the same price on the hotel's website as on a third party site, book directly. If you can get a substantially better deal on a third party website, perhaps because of a coupon code or an air+hotel package, you may want to consider the opportunity cost to get your points and benefits. It may well be worth booking via the third party and saving cash.

Nearly all hotel websites offer some sort of best rate guarantee. However, I have found them to be very hit and miss. None of them accept screenshots as proof. They need to "independently verify" the claim on their own timeline, which may be 1-2 days. This is plenty of time for that better rate to disappear on its own. That's frustrating when you want the points and elite night credits, but know that the guarantee may be denied and then you have nothing. If you can book a cancelable third party rate, however, then it is usually worth booking that and attempting to use the best rate guarantee to book directly. Then you can cancel the third party booking. If it's denied, you can choose if you want to simply use that third-party booking.

# CHAPTER 8

# Credit Card Points / Transferable Currencies: Your Most Important Tool

This is definitely one of the most important chapters in being able to book more fantastic award travel.

Many people make the mistake of accruing their miles with one airline. In many cases it's because they only earn miles from flying. It's perfectly fine to credit all your flying miles to one program if you don't fly a ton. In fact, that makes sense. But when it comes to credit cards, that is a whole other ballgame.

You see, many people decide that because they fly a particular airline a lot, they should also have that airline's credit card. And it may make sense to get that card for the benefits it provides, but it rarely, if ever, makes sense to put your day to day spending on that card.

"But," you protest, "by charging everything on my Delta credit card, I accumulate more Delta miles."

Sure, but what happens when you want an award flight and the only availability is on United? You can't use your Delta miles for United flights. But if you had some Chase

Ultimate Rewards points, you could transfer them to United and book the flight.

"Fine," you say, begrudgingly, "But what if Delta did actually have a flight available?" Then you could book those flights via Skyteam partners Air France or Korean Air, or Delta partner Virgin Atlantic with those same Chase Ultimate Rewards points. Or you could transfer another transferable currency to Delta.

So now that I've opened this chapter with an example, I'll go back and define the term "Transferable Currency." Transferable currency refers to a point that can be moved, or transferred, from that program into a frequent flyer mile. Right now, there are 4 major transferable currencies:

> Chase *Ultimate Rewards*
> American Express *Membership Rewards*
> Citi *ThankYou*
> Starwood Hotels: *Starwood Preferred Guest* (a.k.a SPG)

Importantly, the first three are banks, while the last one is actually the Starwood hotel chain's loyalty program. But I count SPG as a Transferable Currency because you can both earn the points with a credit card (The Starwood Preferred Guest credit cards from American Express) and transfer them out to a massive number of airlines, including some that none of the other three partner with.

Each of these programs have a range of airlines you can transfer to, as well as a few hotel programs.

American Express has 14 airline partners and 3 hotel partners, Chase has 7 airline partners and 4 hotel partners, Citi has 13 airline partners, and SPG has 34 airline partners.

And you can, of course, redeem SPG for all Starwood and Marriott hotels as well!

I maintain a list of transfer partners and transfer ratios at http://milestalk.com/transfer-partners/.

In Chapter 4, I talked a lot about goal setting. This is a great time to double back on that and see which airlines you are most likely to fly on, and see which programs will be easiest to transfer to. It's also a good time to revisit Award Hacker to see what airline programs will be best for your travel goals.

There are some things to keep an eye on. For instance, SPG is the only possible transfer partner for a whopping 16 airlines. Also noteworthy is that Singapore Airlines partners with all four transferable currencies. That means that, even if you can't get enough points in one program for the award you want, you may be able to get enough in multiple programs and combine them. Try that when you are only collecting miles with one airline!

Another consideration is transfer time. Some airlines will put a flight on hold while you transfer your points over, but others won't. Given that award availability can quite literally appear and vanish by the minute, this is an important consideration in deciding which transferable currencies you acquire and how you use them.

Chase and American Express transfer nearly instantly to most of their partners. So you can be quick to transfer and snag an award. Citi can take up to a week or more to complete a transfer and SPG's vary quite a bit. So while in some cases you will be able to hold an award and transfer, other strategies may involve figuring out a pattern of availability with an airline, transferring the points speculatively, and waiting to jump on something that works. If you aren't comfortable with that, you may opt to limit your strategy to Chase/Amex transfer partners. Each program and transfer partner varies, but an online search for "How long does X take to transfer to Y?" will yield reliable results. Be sure that the post or message is fairly recent.

Here is the ultimate point about transferable currencies: Because award availability is often stingy, you never want to be tied into one program. If having miles in various frequent flyer mile programs is diversification, then transferable currency is the ultimate diversification plan, because you have exponentially more options with each transferable currency.

# CHAPTER 9

# High-End Credit Cards: You Can Get More Than You Give

If you are like me, you have a "thing" against paying annual fees on credit cards. The concept just doesn't sit right.

But in recent years I've really gotten my head around paying annual fees, as long as I'm getting more in value than I am paying for the fee.

And so the reality now is that I pay annual fees on several cards each year. And I come out ahead.

Right now, three of the major premium cards are the Chase Sapphire Reserve, the Citi Prestige, and the Platinum Card from American Express.

There are also super-premium cards like the fabled "Black Card" (actually called the Centurion and issued by American Express) but I won't discuss those here because a) they aren't accessible to most people and b) because in a cost/benefit analysis, they come out on the losing end most of the time because of their outsized annual fees.

The premium cards all have annual fees in the $400-$600 range. There are also many other cards with annual fees ranging from \$50-\$200. A great many of these have annual benefits that can make them worth carrying, ranging from a complimentary status level as long as you hold the card, to a free annual hotel night, up to a free companion airline ticket each year, which can handily beat the annual fee in one fell swoop.

You will need to do your own math to see if a particular card is worth it for you. Below, I've created a simple worksheet you can use to see if you will come out ahead or behind with a particular card. If you still aren't sure after doing the worksheet, that's a good time to come to MilesTalk.com or one of its social channels (Facebook/Twitter) to ask for help.

First, I'll show you my example of a cost-benefit analysis for myself with the Chase Sapphire Reserve card. Below that, you'll find a worksheet you can use yourself.

It's important to realize that different people will value things differently. It's never purely about what a benefit is worth but, rather, what it is worth *to you*.

## *Chase Sapphire Reserve Cost/Benefit Analysis*

(Fees/benefits are as of November 2017 and subject to change - this is meant as an example analysis only.)

Card annual fee: $450

|   | Benefit | My Value | Notes |
|---|---------|----------|-------|
| A | $300 Annual Travel Credit (good on any travel including air, hotel, car rental, parking, parking meters, taxi, tolls, Uber/Lyft) | $300 | I probably spend $300 on these categories in a month. Easy. |
| B | Priority Pass Lounge Access | $100 | It includes Priority Pass lounge access for me and unlimited guests with no per-visit fee. While worth more than $100 to buy the same, I lower the value because a) I can live without lounge access and b) I get it from other Premium cards. This is very subjective. |
| C | Global Entry reimbursement | $100 in year 1, $0 thereafter. Value at $20 | You can only get this once every 5 years. For simplicity, I'll amortize over 5 years at $20 a year. |

| | | | |
|---|---|---|---|
| D | Primary car rental insurance | $50 | This is actually a major benefit if you own a car, carry your own insurance, but rent cars often. Primary CDW (Collission Damage Waiver) and LDW (Loss Damage Waiver) means you are 100% covered and will never need to involve your own policy - even for a deductible. |
| E | No Foreign Transaction Fee | $0 | I'm glad it's a feature but most of my travel credit cards offer this. |
| F | Rewards | $250 | Another tricky one. You earn points worth at a minimum 1.5 cents apiece. But with transfer partners and category bonuses of 3x points for all travel and dining, you have a 4.5% cash back card here when you spend on travel and dining and redeem in the portal. An average card is 1-2%. How much you value this depends on your annual spending on travel and dining. I'm assuming I spend $10,000 a year there and compared to a 2% cash back card come out $250 ahead ($10,000 at 4.5% vs $10,000 at 2% in rewards). I'll do even better if I transfer points to airlines/hotels. |

| G | Signup bonus value | $750 | The current bonus is 50,000 Ultimate Rewards points which are worth a minimum of $750 when redeemed through the Chase travel portal. Use this only in calculating your year one value. |
|---|---|---|---|
| H | Total Year One Value | $1,470 | Add lines A-G |
|   | Total Year 2 and beyond value | $720 | Subtract line G |
|   | Am I ahead or behind? | $270 | Subtract annual fee. If it's not negative, you could do well with this card. If it's negative, you may be better off without this card. |

## Blank Credit Card Annual Fee Cost/ Benefit Analysis Worksheet

Card annual fee: _____

|   | Benefit | My Value | Notes |
|---|---------|----------|-------|
| A |  |  |  |
| B |  |  |  |
| C |  |  |  |
| D |  |  |  |
| E |  |  |  |
| F |  |  |  |
| G | Signup bonus value |  |  |
| H | Total Year One Value |  | Add lines A-G |
|   | Total Year 2 and beyond value |  | Subtract line G |
|   | Am I ahead or behind? |  | Subtract annual fee. If it's not negative, you could do well with this card. If it's negative, you may be better off without this card. |

You can download a copy of this sheet at
http://milestalk.com/annual-fee-worksheet/

CHAPTER 10

# Credit Card Sign-Up Bonuses:
# Fill Your Points Coffers Quickly

t's no secret that one of the most lucrative ways to get a windfall of miles is a new travel rewards credit card. While the bonuses change constantly (making it useless to mention any specific card bonuses here), they can be massive, sometimes up to 100,000 miles or points or more! I've personally earned well over a million miles just from credit card signup bonuses.

If you have good credit, you should absolutely open some new cards from time to time to take advantage of the bonus offers. But you should also do your research. The offers for the exact same card can vary wildly. One day it could be 30,000 miles for opening a card and spending a certain amount in a few months. But the next day it could be 60,000 miles for the exact same spend requirement. It's always a good idea to search around before you apply. "XYZ card best signup offer" should yield you some good reference points in an online search.

Because you obviously cannot open a new card every day (see the section at the end of this chapter on Bank Restrictions),

I recommend making a list of the cards you want and historical bonus offers and crafting a strategy for which cards you want to get when the signup offer is at or near a historical high. Your overall travel goal strategy will also factor in here, though, because you may be more concerned with getting one kind of transferable currency as opposed to another, for example. If you apply in the wrong order, you may wind up not getting approved for some cards you really want.

I'll also take this opportunity to mention that I have links to current credit card offers at http://milestalk.com/credit-cards/.

I greatly appreciate it if you use my links when you apply if, and only if, they are the best possible offers available for you. I may receive a commission from the card issuer if you are approved and that will enable me to spend the time to write more books like this as well as update this one regularly.

## Effect on Your Credit Score

You should only be doing any of this if you have good credit. While that is subjective, I'll say that means a score above 680 as a guideline. If you are below that, focus on making on-time payments with your existing cards, reducing balances to zero, and then come back to this.

If you have a good credit score, you will no doubt wonder what effect applying for a new card will have on it. In my experience, if you already have good credit, you'll lose about 7 points on your score and get them back about 3 months later. You should be prepared that you may lose more than that, even up to 20 points. But they will come back.

Keep in mind that there are many factors that are used to calculate your credit score. For instance, a new card with a big limit (that you don't put to much use) will increase both your overall credit line as well as lower your debt utilization ratio. This lower credit line utilization ratio should boost your score long term.

That said, there's no exact rule on the effect of one or more card applications and I am in no way giving you financial advice here. If you have any concerns about this at all, consult a professional.

## Bank Restrictions On New Card Accounts

If you're new to miles and points, you may not be aware that you can no longer apply for credit cards all day long and get approved just because you have good credit. For instance, Chase is known to enforce a rule dubbed "5/24" which means that you won't be approved for most Chase cards, though there are exceptions, if you have opened 5 new credit cards within the last 24 months. This means that if you are new to this, you may want to get your Chase cards first. American Express may limit you to 5 of their credit products, which are your personal and small business cards combined.

You will also want to always read the fine print on bonus eligibility. Each issuer has some standard practices on getting repeat bonuses for the same card product. As of this moment, Chase will give you a bonus if it's been 24 months since you last got one on the same card. American Express will only give you a bonus once-per-lifetime-per-card. Citi follows a more complex rule where you can't get a bonus if you have opened, or closed, a card in the same rewards product family within the last 24 months. Bank of America limits you to 2 of their own cards within 2 months, 3 total within a year, and 4 total within 2 years.

Because of all of these complexities, strategizing your card sign up strategy in advance is crucial.

## <u>A Note on Credit Cards</u>

While travel rewards credit cards are without question the easiest way to rack up miles, it's important to note the pitfalls.

Rewards credit cards tend to carry the ***absolute highest interest rates*** of any card category. It's people that carry balances at excess of 20% APR that pay for the rewards.

Don't be that guy or gal paying for the rewards for everyone else. If you cannot pay your credit card bills in full, every month, do not open more cards than you can pay in full. Even that big bonus will not be worth it if you are paying 20% interest.

If this is you, please pay off what you owe first and then, and only then, start with this aspect of frequent flyer miles.

# CHAPTER 11

# Credit Card Category Spend Bonuses: Don't Leave Points on the Table

M any people think that, once you get your big sign up bonuses, you've topped out on your ability to earn major miles. But if you put even a few thousand dollars a month of your normal monthly expenses on the right cards, the bonuses can really add up. The key is knowing which cards have the best category spend bonuses for your spending habits and then using the right card for the right bonuses.

First, let's look at some common categories for bonus spend:

- Supermarkets
- Airfare/hotel
- Dining
- Gas
- Office Supplies
- Phone and Cable

- Everything else

Now let's compare some of the "best in category" cards to the 1-2% cash that you are getting if you use one card for everything. Note that many of the cards below do have annual fees, so the math in the premium cards chapter can also be applied here.

- Supermarkets: 6x on American Express Blue Cash
- Airfare/hotel: 5x on American Express Platinum / 3x on Citi Prestige and Premier / 3x on Chase Sapphire Reserve
- Dining: 3x on Chase Sapphire Reserve
- Gas: 3x on Citi ThankYou Prestige and Premier cards
- Office Supplies: 5x on Ink Cash for Business
- Phone and Cable: 5x on Ink Cash for Business
- Everything else: 1.5x on Chase Freedom Unlimited (worth 2.25%) or 2% cash back card

Now, to show you the power of the multiplier, let's map out how we'd fare if we used a good bonus category spend card for each category across a year of spending. I'm going to assume total yearly spend of $50,000 to keep things simple.

- Supermarkets: $5,000 on Blue Cash = 30,000 American Express Membership Rewards
- Airfare/hotel: $4,000 on American Express Platinum = 20,000 Membership Rewards OR on Citi Prestige / Premier = 12,000 Citi ThankYou points OR on Chase Sapphire Reserve = 12,000 Ultimate Rewards points

- Dining: $8,000 (if you live in a major city, this is not high!) on Chase Sapphire Reserve = 24,000 Ultimate Rewards points
- Gas: $2,000 on Citi Prestige or Premier = 6,000 Citi ThankYou points
- Office Supplies: $2,000 on Chase Ink Cash = 10,000 Ultimate Rewards points
- Phone and Cable: $2,500 on Chase Ink Cash = 12,500 Ultimate Rewards points
- Everything else: $22,500 on Chase Freedom Unlimited = 33,750 Ultimate Rewards points

If you had spent $50,000 on a 1% cash back or rewards card, you'd have earned $500. Let's see how we did with our strategy. For simplicity, in categories with multiple options, I've chosen one based on maximizing earnings across all three rewards programs.

- 30,000 American Express Membership Rewards
- 18,000 Citi ThankYou points
- 80,250 Chase Ultimate Rewards points

You are now looking at over $2,000 worth of points for your yearly spend, versus the $500 you'd have gotten from a 1% cash back card or (if you were already pretty smart about cash back) $1,000 from a 2% cash back card. At the very least, this doubled your yearly rewards. But if you use the points wisely, you can do even better than that. Don't forget to factor in your annual fees, but if you used the worksheet in Chapter 9 for each card, then you are only using cards you are above breakeven with regards to the annual fees.

CHAPTER 12 ✈

# Earn Points and Miles by Banking: Make your $ Work For You

There are currently two ways you can earn transferable points and miles with your bank accounts.

Citi will give you a small monthly ThankYou point bonus, depending on your banking relationship with them. The amount of points you earn will vary based on which account you have and which products you have as well, for instance Citi Priority with Direct Deposit and Bill Payment will earn 800 points a month. That's 9,600 a year for doing what you were already doing.

Citi also sometimes has offers for a new account bonus. Offers of 50,000 ThankYou points are not uncommon.

BankDirect.com is an online bank that partners with American Airlines to award AAdvantage miles monthly based on what amount you have on deposit. It used to award nearly unlimited miles, but several years ago they capped earning rates such that only the first $50,000 on deposit in a checking account earns the maximum rate of 100 miles per $1,000 on deposit per month. Your first $50,000 in a savings account earns 50 miles per $1,000. Rates drop to 25 miles per $1,000 over those amounts and you can only have one of each account per household.

Still, a deposit of $50,000 in both checking and savings will award 7,500 AAdvantage miles per month. Compare that against standard liquid savings account which, for many years now, have earned about 1%. You would earn $600 or 90,000 miles (worth $1,200 or more). The kicker? The miles are not taxed as income. You could either have $600 cash and pay tax on that or $1,200 + worth of miles and not pay tax. If you collect AAdvantage miles and have liquid cash anyway, this is a great way to earn an extra 90,000 miles a year.

If you create an account, Bank Direct will give you 1,000 bonus miles if you have a referral from a friend and the referrer gets 1,000 miles as well. You are more than welcome to email me at dave@milestalk.com and I'll refer you.

# CHAPTER 13

# Earning Miles / Points / Cash Back for Eating and Shopping

This one is so easy, yet so many people leave the proverbial cash on the table by not doing the little bit of work to earn miles and points for these activities.

Earning miles for eating out is the easiest one by far. Just pick your favorite frequent flyer program, go to their website, find their section on Earning Miles, and sign up. You link all of your credit cards into the site and when you eat at any participating restaurant, you'll automatically be awarded the points. Sure, you can go out of your way to eat only at participating restaurants, but even if you just "see what sticks" you will likely earn thousands of free miles each year.

Here are a few of the major program links:

American Airlines: https://aa.rewardsnetwork.com
United Airlines: https://dining.mileageplus.com
Delta Air Lines: https://skymiles.rewardsnetwork.com
Southwest: https://www.rapidrewardsdining.com
JetBlue: https://truebluedining.com

Alaska Airlines:
https://mileageplan.rewardsnetwork.com

Most also have a signup bonus of 1,000 - 3,000 miles.

More interesting, and more rewarding, are the shopping portals. Just by clicking a link from a particular shopping portal to the merchant you were going to order from anyway, you can earn cash back or miles or points, sometimes up to 25% or more of your purchase price! These rebates even work on merchandise where the manufacturer doesn't allow the store to offer discounts.

You can earn straight cash back at a site like Ebates.com, miles from any major airline, or even Chase Ultimate Rewards or Citi ThankYou points.

The biggest thing to know about the shopping portals is that they will all pay different rates for each store and will change their rates on a daily basis. So for one store, a cashback site may pay 5% one day and 20% the next, while at the same time a mileage earning portal may pay 20 miles per dollar one day and then just 3 miles per dollar the next.

Here's a list of the most common North America based shopping portals that earn miles and points:

Chase's "Shop Through Chase" Shopping Portal (earn Ultimate Rewards points):
https://www.chase.com/ccp/index.jsp?pg_name=ccpmapp/shared/marketing/page/chase-ultimate-rewards

Marriott Shop Your Way:
https://mrewards.shopmyway.com/earnpoints/home

Air Canada: https://www.aeroplan.com/estore/

Alaska Airlines:
https://www.alaskaair.com/MileagePlanShopping/

American Airlines:
https://www.aadvantageeshopping.com

British Airways: https://www.shopping.ba.com

Delta Air Lines: https://www.skymilesshopping.com

JetBlue: https://shoptrue.jetblue.com

Southwest:
https://rapidrewardsshopping.southwest.com

United Airlines: https://shopping.mileageplus.com

There are sites to track all of your options, which seem to become more numerous by the day. Cashback Monitor (https://www.cashbackmonitor.com) does a great job of showing you, at a glance, what all of your potential portal earnings are for a particular store.

# CHAPTER 14

# Useful Websites to Bookmark

First, here are links to all of the various ways you can follow and get support from MilesTalk. Daily tips are posted to the blog as well as Facebook and Twitter. Get your travel inspiration from the Instagram feed. And you can ask any question you've got in the private Facebook group.

Website: http://MilesTalk.com

Facebook page:
https://www.facebook.com/MilesTalkDave/

Private MilesTalk Facebook Group:
https://www.facebook.com/groups/MilesTalk/

Twitter and Instagram: @MilesTalk

Current signup bonuses for travel rewards credit cards can always be found at http://MilesTalk.com/credit-cards/. Please know that I may receive a commission when you use my links to apply for credit cards and will greatly appreciate your support. Think of it as a virtual tip jar.

Below are links to key resources I've mentioned throughout the book.

ExpertFlyer.com - Paid service for award availability searches and alerts

AwardHacker.com - Find out how much a route costs to redeem from all possible loyalty programs

WhereToCredit.com - Using an airline and fare class, find out how many miles you'd earn crediting the flight to various programs

StatusMatcher.com - Lists successful and unsuccessful attempts to status match elite statuses

Google.com/flights - For easily finding the best airline routes and prices from any city or region to another

CashbackMonitor.com - Locate the best cashback options for a particular store at that moment.

Ebates.com - For cashback (miles and points have to be earned through their respective portals)

**Disclaimer:** *All banks, credit card products, airlines, and hotel brands are trademarks of their respective owners. Nothing within this book constitutes an endorsement of any particular product or service. For certain websites that I link to, I use an affiliate link where available that may earn me a referral* *credit. These links in no way alter the price of any of those services to you and are in no way the reason I list any of those sites in this book.*

# CHAPTER 15

# Tying It All Together

've done my very best to introduce you to the world of miles and points in a way that is easily actionable. I encourage you to set your first travel goal now. Map it out and determine how you will achieve it.

Hopefully, you will have questions. Once you've absorbed everything in this book, you can harness groupthink by asking questions not just on MilesTalk.com, but also on Twitter and Instagram (@MilesTalk) and on the private MilesTalk group on Facebook at https://facebook.com/groups/MilesTalk/

Like anything worth doing, this hobby takes some dedication and some will not think it is worth the effort. That just means there are that many more miles for you!

Nearly every day I speak to someone that, just a year ago, wasn't even bothering to credit flights to a frequent flyer program and, after realizing the power of miles and points, has already had their first experience at the pointy end of the plane thanks to miles and points.

You're next!

# ABOUT THE AUTHOR

Since 2003, Dave Grossman has collected literally **millions and millions** of **frequent flyer miles and hotel points**. He's flown around the world in **first class seats** that would cost **$29,000** using frequent flyer miles and a few bucks in tax. And he's stayed in some of the finest hotels – *often for free,* thanks to miles and points!

Dave's hosted two seminars on miles and points at *South By Southwest* in Austin, and he's been quoted in the *Wall Street Journal* and *Travel + Leisure*, published on Bravo TV's *JetSet* website, and has spoken on the *Condé Nast Traveler* podcast series. He also writes the blog *MilesTalk.com* which helps readers learn how to earn and spend miles and points to travel better.

Follow him at:

Web: MilesTalk.com
Instagram: @MilesTalk
Twitter: @MilesTalk
Facebook Page: /MilesTalkDave
Private Facebook Group: "MilesTalk"

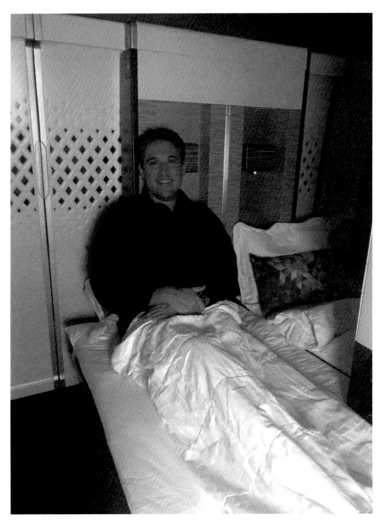

Ready for bed in the Etihad First Class Apartment

Etihad First Class Apartment

.

Made in the USA
Lexington, KY
22 April 2018